W9-BAL-210

Gymnastics

BY ALLAN MOREY

AMICUS HIGH INTEREST · AMICUS INK

Amicus High Interest and Amicus Ink are imprints of Amicus
P.O. Box 1329, Mankato, MN 56002
www.amicuspublishing.us

Library of Congress Cataloging-in-Publication Data
Morey, Allan.
 Gymnastics / by Allan Morey.
    pages cm. – (Summer Olympic sports)
Includes index.
Summary: "Presents information about gymnastics in the
Olympics, including different kinds of gymnastic events,
well-known gymnasts such as Gabrielle Douglas, and how
gymnastics in the Olympics works today"– Provided by
publisher.
ISBN 978-1-60753-808-0 (library binding)
ISBN 978-1-60753-897-4 (ebook)
ISBN 978-1-68152-049-0 (paperback)
1. Gymnastics–Juvenile literature. 2. Olympics–Juvenile
literature. I. Title.
GV461.3.M67 2016
796.44–dc23

                              2014045800

Editor: Wendy Dieker
Series Designer: Kathleen Petelinsek
Book Designer: Aubrey Harper
Photo Researcher: Derek Brown

Photo Credits: Troy Wayrynen/ZUMA Press/Corbis cover;
Bruce Chambers/ZUMA Press/Corbis 5; Ian MacNicol/Getty
Images 6; PCN/Corbis 9; Wang Lei/Xinhua Press/Corbis
10; Alan Edwards/Alamy 13; Gero Breloer/epa/Corbis 14;
Associated Press 17; Vernon Bryant/Dallas Morning News/
Corbis 18; Jeff Siner/Charlotte Observer/MCT/Getty Images
20-21; Julian Finney/Getty Images 23; Li Ziheng/Xinhua Press/
Corbis 24; Julie Jacobson/AP/Corbis 26-27; Brian Peterson/
ZUMA Press/Corbis 29

HC 10 9 8 7 6 5 4 3 2
PB 10 9 8 7 6 5 4 3 2 1

Table of Contents

Going for the Gold

The Summer Olympic Games are held every four years. The world's best athletes meet. They all want a gold medal. But only the best will get it.

What's one of the most popular events? Gymnastics. Some gymnasts do tumbling moves. They flip and twist in the air. Others dance with a **prop**. They toss balls and spin hoops. Still others leap sky-high on a trampoline.

US gymnast Gabby Douglas competes on the uneven bars at the 2012 Olympics.

Rhythmic gymnasts use props such as ribbons to dazzle the crowds.

Gymnastics was one of the first Olympic sports. But at that time, it was only for men. Rope climbing was one early **event**. Times have changed. Today, both men and women compete. You will see three styles of gymnastics. The most popular is artistic. You will also see rhythmic gymnastics and trampoline.

Artistic Gymnastics

Artistic gymnasts are tumblers. They go way beyond cartwheels and somersaults, though. These gymnasts do a **routine** on an **apparatus**, or piece of equipment. Flip! Leap! Twist! Judges score them on how well they do a routine. But they also get scored on what they do. Harder moves get higher scores.

US gymnast Jacob Dalton
shows strength on the rings.

Flipping over the vault table is one of four events women do.

 Q Who is the best female gymnast in history?

Women have four events. Each one is on a different piece of equipment. Women spring over a vault table. They tumble across a mat in the floor exercise. On the balance beam, they leap and twist. They spin around the uneven bars. The best woman in each event wins the gold.

Russian gymnast Larisa Latynina. She won 18 medals from 1956 to 1964. That's more than any other gymnast.

Men have six events. Like the women, men spring over the vault. They also do a floor exercise. Instead of the uneven bars, men spin and turn on the parallel bars and the high bar. They whip their legs around on the pommel horse. They show upper body strength on the rings.

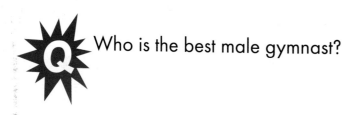
Who is the best male gymnast?

Gold medalist Kohei Uchimura from Japan competes on the high bar.

Some say Vitaly Scherbo. He won six gold medals in 1992. That's more than any other gymnast in one Olympics!

US gymnast Carly Patterson (right) shows off one of the three medals she won in 2004.

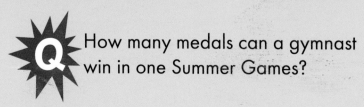
How many medals can a gymnast win in one Summer Games?

Only a few gymnasts make it to the Olympics. At the games, they first do the **qualifying round**. The best gymnasts go on to the **individual event** finals. The ones who do the best in all the events also do the **all-around event**. These gymnasts do each event once more. Some gymnasts are very busy!

 A gymnast could win one for each artistic event, one for all-around, and one for team. That's up to six for women and eight for men!

The biggest prize is the all–around gold medal. Some of the most famous gymnasts have won it. Nadia Comaneci is from Romania. She won in 1976. She is also the first woman to get a perfect 10. US gymnast Gabby Douglas won the gold in 2012. Kohei Uchimura is from Japan. He took silver in 2008. But then he won the gold in 2012.

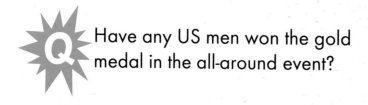

Have any US men won the gold medal in the all-around event?

Famous Romanian gymnast Nadia Comaneci competes on the balance beam in 1980.

 Yes! Two have. Julius Lenhart won gold in 1904. Paul Hamm won in 2004.

The US women's team huddles up during the 2012 Olympics.

Artistic gymnastics also includes a **team event**. The top 12 teams in the world compete at the qualifying round. Each team has five people. Only eight teams move on to the finals. In the finals, the team chooses three gymnasts to perform in each event. The scores are added up. The team with the highest score wins.

Which country has the best team? Russia does. They have the most team medals. But other countries have good teams too. China's men's team won the gold in 2000, 2008, and 2012. The Chinese women won the team gold in 2008. The US women's team won gold in 2012.

Yang Wei of China helped his team win gold in 2000 and 2008.

Rhythmic Gymnastics

A rhythmic gymnast is like a dancer with props. Only women compete. They spin hoops. They toss balls and clubs. They even twirl ribbons. This sport became part of the Olympics in 1984.

Gymnasts do four routines, one for each prop. Their four scores are added up. The gymnast with the highest score wins the gold.

A rhythmic gymnast uses a ball in one of her four routines.

This team from China uses hoops and clubs in their group event.

Q Which team has won the most medals?

In 1996, a rhythmic group event was added to the Summer Games. Each team has five women. Groups perform twice, using one or two of the props.

The group event is fun to watch. Five athletes dance together like ballerinas. As they do, they pass balls. They dive through hoops. It is truly amazing!

 Russia has the most. They have four gold medals and one bronze.

Trampoline

Trampoline is the newest gymnastic event. It became part of the Summer Games in 2000. Both men and women do ten sky-high jumps. They twist, flip, and somersault during each jump. They are scored on how hard the moves are and how high they jump.

Japanese gymnast Yasuhiro Ueyama does a back flip on the trampoline.

26

Cheer Them On!

The moves gymnasts do are amazing. They flip. They spin and twirl. They jump high into the air. Every four years, the Summer Olympics bring us the best in the world. We get to watch the gymnasts wow the crowds with their incredible skills. Cheer for your favorite athletes!

US gymnast Kyla Ross thrills fans with her routine in 2012.

Glossary

all-around event A competition in which gymnasts perform on all the apparatuses.

apparatus A piece of equipment on which gymnasts do routines.

event In gymnastics, a competition on one or more apparatuses.

individual event A competition in which gymnasts compete against each other on just one piece of equipment.

prop An object or element used in rhythmic gymnastics; clubs, hoops, ribbons, and balls are used in the Olympics.

qualifying round The round to determine who will be in the final competition.

routine In gymnastics, a series of movements or skills that get scored.

team event A competition in which athletes compete as a team.

Read More

Gifford, Clive. *Gymnastics*. Mankato, Minn.: Amicus, 2012.

LeBoutillier, Nate. *Gymnastics*. Mankato, Minn.: Creative Education, 2012.

Wood, Alix. *You Can Be a Gymnast*. New York: Gareth Stevens Pub., 2014.

Websites

International Gymnastics Federations
http://www.fig-gymnastics.com

Olympics
http://www.olympic.org

USA Gymnastics
https://usagym.org

Index

About the Author

Allan Morey was never an Olympic athlete, but he
has always enjoyed sports, from playing basketball to
going to baseball games and watching football on TV.
His favorite summer sports are volleyball and disc golf.
Morey writes books for children and lives in St. Paul,
Minnesota, with his family and dog, Ty.